BLOOMING SCARS

BLOOMING SCARS

Words of love, loss and longing

HUMA ADNAN

Copyright © 2020 by Huma Adnan

BLOOMING SCARS

No part of this publication may be reproduced, distributed, or transmitted in any form or by any means, including photocopying, recording, or other electronic or mechanical methods, without the prior written permission of the author except in brief quotations embodied in critical reviews, citations, and literary journals for non-commercial uses permitted by copyright law.

For permission request email the author. humaadnan87@hotmail.com

ISBN: 978-0-9979824-1-1

To
love,
pain
&
survival.

Foreword

I never thought I would be able to write something for someone, other than myself. I have spent much of my life in a corporate environment in various roles within the organisation. I am a writer and I love to travel. I am an amateur photographer and a hopeless romantic. I've seen, felt and experienced life's betrayals as close as possible. Life's twists don't amaze me anymore. The flow is the path and that I've come to terms with.

You cross paths with people in your life for a reason, maybe to support them throughout or just be present for the time when they eventually need you. I was introduced to Huma in not the best of circumstances and now after so many years having passed it still seems like yesterday how our dreams shattered and what it took for her to stand back up and not give up hope. I know Huma to be a fighter, strong-willed and resilient. Life, a mystery unfolds every second in front of our eyes and I've often seen her standing, gazing for its next move to be ready. She has been broken, brought down to her knees and yet here she is, unfazed by all of it, restarting a new chapter, her fourth book – a journey of losing love and finding the strength to love again. This book will take on you a journey of a broken heart and beyond and will bring you right back to the start, where you are full of hope.

Huma has been a light for me in times when I had given up on chasing my dreams. She teaches me to be humble and caring and to fight what you want in life. And for that I thank her, for being in touch as often as she could, for guiding me through the dark and towards the light and being a friend when I needed the most. I hope someday I will have the opportunity to be there for her as she was for me.

Mohammed Abrar Ahmed
Author of
Daydreams and Midnight Realities
& The Years Gone By

Contents

Love Flies — 1

You are a Survivor! — 2

We are Finding.. — 4

If Only Semantics was Enough — 6

Departure — 8

RIP — 10

Sapiosexual — 13

A Hopeless Hope — 16

Humzad 18

Equally 20

Loving the Damaged 21

Platonic Love 23

Japanese Knotweed 26

Before We Part 28

Falling in Love Again 30

Dreams 32

Broken Union 35

24 Aug 2018 37

A Toast 39

Love as if.. 41

Ode to a Lost Lover

42

I Carry You

44

Transitory

46

Love Them

47

Stolen Moments

48

Fragile

50

Spring in Love's Autumn

52

Prayers

54

Heart is at Home

55

The World Remembers Us

58

My Darling

59

Dissolving in Ashes

61

Ode to My Ex Best Friend

62

Soul Communicating with Body

64

It's All Possible with Love

67

Shajarat Al Hayat- The Tree of Life

68

Soberly Drunk

69

Shelter

71

Set Yourself Free

72

Teach Us The Art of Growing

73

Reborn

74

One Day

77

Questions

78

Words I Believed in

81

Confession 82

Despite the Efforts 84

Question Loneliness 85

Right Timings 88

My Methadone 89

It's Clear Now 91

Dollhouse 92

Warriors 95

Depression 96

Too Late 100

The Song of Demons 101

Save Thyself 103

Girl with Purple Hair

104

New World

107

To Phoebus

109

To Old Me

111

Together We Will

114

Tale of an Expat

115

Irreplaceable

119

In the Air

120

Broken House

121

The Poem in the Times of Corona 1

122

Empty Mansion

123

I Failed..

124

Human Presence 126

We Will Heal 127

Love Desires 129

Depression Hits Again 130

Home 132

Expedition 134

Familiarity 135

Nani's (Grandma) Lessons Don't Work 136

Moment 138

Manual 139

Rules 140

On Words 143

Poem in the times of Corona 2

146

The Only Prayer

149

Soulship

150

Loud Whispers!

155

Love Flies

How terrifying it is
To know that what seems today
Strong, passionate and
Sincerest love,
Will have no existence
Tomorrow.

You are a Survivor!

One day,
Take out time and visit the places
Where you lived
during the most crucial stages of your life.
Recall the days of struggle,
Look at the roads where you walked
Fighting back tears.
Go and stare at the walls of the house,
Which hide your screams.
See the ground
Where you dropped yourself many times.
After all the flashbacks,
Smile!
Praise the Lord for bringing you
Out of the darkness.
Praise Him for taking away
That haunted time.
As today you are
A living legend.
For you are special!
Be proud!
Be strong!

Since not everyone gets to feel the pain.
Because not everyone
Comes out of storm
Like a survivor!

We are Finding..

In his soul
I poured mine.
Heart rode on the waves
Untamed and wild.
And charade became
Impossible to hide.
I confessed love
And he was silent.
I started to walk,
He held my hand
And repeated my words
With addition of 'too.'
I believed it.
My particles,
Atoms,
Neurons,
All became his property
Before I could have known.
My every cell, tissue and,
Organ was falling in love.
I was me,
But I wasn't.

He was mine,
Yet he wasn't.
In return for my love,
I was given
Friendship,
Fondness
And care.
But not love.
Since he had loved
And he lost the spark.
No matter how high the flames of my heart were,
He couldn't love me back.
He couldn't call me home.
Today,
We both are nomads.
I, in search of him.
He, in search of her.

If Only Semantics was Enough

I wish
There were words good enough to explain
How demons can hold us from a throat at 2 am.
I wish there were phrases clear enough to tell
How whispering makes us do things that we least wish to do.
We push people,
We bleed ourselves,
We claw our skins,
We become monsters with no life breathing inside.
We wish to say,
"Stay!
Hold me!
Talk to me!
Look into my eyes!
Leave the phone
And listen to me!"
Or
"I am scared, just be with me!"
We wish to say,
"Call me and let me cry

While I hear your voice!"
We want to scream,
"For this moment leave all that is waiting and sit beside me!"
But instead we say-
"I'm all right.
You can go."
And what we can never tell, once we are left alone
The demons, the whispering, the traumas
Set us on fire and dance around us and eat our flesh!
They feast on us till the sun rises.
And we go to work with swollen eyes
Unable to explain
Why- why- our eyes keep losing the soul.
When you say recite the holy verses
We look at the holy book in our hands and wonder
Is depression the karma of sins?
We -who after showing you
Our darkest corners are left alone-
die before death approaches us.
I wish there were
Enough sentences-
Literary devices-
Strong adjectives to explain
The survivors, the crestfallen
The depressed, the dispirited
Deserve to be loved.

Departure

4 am flights and the airports give me anxiety.
They give *you* stress.
Tomorrow morning when I will wake up
You would have gone.
Because you hate goodbyes at the airport
And I like dreams more than reality.
I would pretend to sleep,
But after every minute
I would go on google and type "AC936 flight status"
And then would stare at my screen and imagine you
Flying 24 thousand feet above me.

I would despise the map for some time for being so much of ocean and so less of the land.

And parting lands through salty waters filled with the tears of people living apart.

The wrinkles of my bed sheet and the seashell lamp beside me will announce you are gone.

As soon as the sun would come out.
I will- - I will embrace it and I won't miss you.
Because 'miss you' is a sad thing.
I will always remember you
Because you are leaving your infinite love behind.

Our roads may cross again, our lips probably lock again.
We might hold each other again,
But till then I shall love you and
You shall love me.

RIP

Last night my friend called me
And before I could have said hello, I heard her sniffing,
Like a rain pouring against a glass pane.
"Hey Simi! Are you okay?"
I sounded calm like the sea,
Since this wasn't the first time she cried.
Last week it was for a cat she found dead by the roadside.
And week before that it was the death of her favorite character from a series.

What is it, hun?
I asked while pouring the milk
And balancing the phone between my ear and shoulder.
"I am in chaos in utter chaos."
So this time she couldn't find the reason to cry, I thought to myself.

I cleared my throat and began
Why don't you have some sleep.
"I can't!" She cut in before I could have showered some wise words.
"I feel..
I feel nothing!
I feel unwanted!

I feel unloved!
I feel broken!
I feel like I exist but I do not!
I breathe but I suffocate!
I – I- - "
This time I cut in-
"Hey! We all love you!
It's just the product of your mind!
It's 12 am and you have a long day ahead!
Pray to- -
"Pray to??"
She lost the temper
And threw words out
As after this eruption
Volcano will be dead!
"I called Raj, he said pray to Krishna!
I talked to Jane and she said, pray to Jesus!
I texted Hassan and he answered pray to Allah.
Tena said I should believe in science
And let a psychiatrist do the work.
But who knows what I need??"
"Alright! I sighed!
Well sleep now and we will figure this out
Tomorrow!"
She put the phone down
Promising that she would go to bed
And leave the mess out of her head.
Proud of myself
I decided to eat a cookie and while munching it I
Smiled- what a great Friend I am!

New morning, new sunrise
I head to work with my mind so light!
I let my fingers dance on keyboard
Until I checked my phone in the afternoon,
"Hey you got the news?
Simi is found dead in her room!
I logged on my Facebook and saw wall filled with her photos posted by mutual friends
Who she hardly ever talked to.
With a caption RIP and I felt my blood gushing through my ears and bursting my heart I wanted to scream,
YOU SAY REST IN PEACE!
But what difference does it make now?
We all need some attention and on virtual world
The death news of a neighbor's dog can get you more likes than you get on a photo you click with your boyfriend.
Or the chocolate cake you had last Sunday.
While they get hearts and thumbs
And sorrowful similes.
I sit back quietly because
I somewhere know,
I ripped her!
But I ask myself
What she needed
That religion and science couldn't give.

Sapiosexual

While people make love on the silk
And find romance
On the wrinkled sheets.
While they explore and touch,
And kiss the curves, the moles, the pores and lips-
I somewhere away
From normal -
From common -
From ordinary -
Sitting among
People,
Pink
White
Blue
Yellow
Colors
While stirring the coffee
And watching the chocolate
Dissolving in hot pouring milk,
Think at the back of my mind
If I could have
A human sitting opposite me

Looking straight into my eyes.
A human who asks me
Hey love! Read what you have written
Or read this!
Or let me read this for you!

He opens his lips and words dance and swirl like honey spreading on a cake.

He reads to me Byron without knowing
His fingers dance on my hand.
I feel the touch
Like a dew drop
That allows a cactus to feel
What it is to be a rose.
The rose dies yet fragrance stays.
And that touch
Tells me the night is only for lovers
Who seek bodies and days are for people like us
Who kiss through rhymes,
Who set the fire on hearts among a coffee steam.
Who whisper..
And talk..
And walk..
And let the walls of the old town envy them.
They forget the crowd
And live in the moment.
Such lovers are made of
Golden dust and some magic.
I can be that someone
Who can light the fire in empty chambers.
I will toss your silk sheet

And make your day
A wild journey,
But if only you were here.
If only you existed.

A Hopeless Hope

I often ask time
Why it had to bring you
When our bodies cannot ignite love.
But body is just a mass
And if I break it into molecules and atoms
And keep them under sunlight,
I would see the colors of you.
All these years I was finding the other half of my soul on ground,
But then I met you amongst the constellations.
But why the Gracious Lord
Keeps us apart when you hurt yourself miles away
And I bleed here?
When your heart cries,
my shoulders soak.
We share-
Heartbeats and the lavender soul.
We are incomplete- like,
A shore without the sea.
And now the atoms, the universe, the soul and heart
Are conspiring to unite our bodies.
But-

Is our union waiting for us
On the other side of this world?

Humzad

The soul has the roots,
They grow,
They sprout,
They turn into saplings
And become a shade tree-
And under those trees
Live
My *Humzad* and *I*.
Humzad, my *Constant Companion.*
To some it's my *spiritual double*
And to others a *human.*
To me he is a
Part of me.
Part of us.
Part who has seen
With me the good and the worse times.
Part who sleeps
When my eyes close.
Part who holds me when
I need him the most.
Part of my soul who grew up,
Lived,

Survived,
And has worn the crown
Of scars
With pride.
Part who is sad
Because I am sad,
Part who is living
Because I am living.
My Humzad
Might be inside my soul,
Heart,
In my home
Or
In a parallel dimension.
And
But what if,
Humzad is not he
But I?

Equally

You were not the first person I loved.
I was not the first person you loved.
You were not the first person whose heart I broke.
I was not the first person whose heart you broke.
It wasn't your first time to ignite an affair with lies.
It wasn't the first time I flirted.
Hence, we reached to the roads
Where we wished to steal each other
And then we both
Ran out of love.
Thus,
Karma hit you.
Karma hit me.

Loving the Damaged

We who fall in love
With wounds,
Broken souls,
Dark pasts.
The hollow bodies.
The shattered glasses,
The demolished buildings,
The bones in the graves,
The abandoned houses.
We who love
To heal, to mend
To grow, to change.
Years and years later
We come home to
Death Chill-
A demised body
With a wilted rose
On its bosom
Waiting to be buried
For decades.
But it doesn't decompose
It is reborn

And it dies.
Reborn
And dies.
Because it made the choice of
Loving
The Graveyards,
The Beasts,
The Cold hearts,
The Broken homes-
This body is not of beloveds
But lovers
Who thought
Their love would make
A difference.
However,
Love died
Because
Darkness was adamant not to
Allow the lights.
The injured was persistent
Not to poultice the wounds.
The unloved
Was firm
Not to accept love.
And lovers,
In the process to love the stones
forgot to breathe -
Since every heart needs
Some oxygen to live.

Platonic Love

He spreads light.
A kind of light which can only be felt by someone special.
I guess I am that special one.
His presence doesn't give me
Butterflies in the stomach.
His touch doesn't arouse me.
It just wraps me like a wax
Around the thread
And I burn slowly in love and glow
In the darkness.
When I say Love-
Don't misunderstand me for the love people make.
I talk of love where eyes meet unintentionally.
Love which brings roses on cheeks.
Love with whom
A single day fight can
Turn the world upside down.
It's a love who hears you quietly.
Love who doesn't remember
To text you when he is with his friends.
Love who is careless
Yet caring.

Love that sparks your eyes
When you are blue.
Love who laughs with you
When you are happy.
Love who laughs more
When you are angry.
Love who understands you
After misunderstanding many times.
Love who makes you mad, says sorry and again makes you mad.
Love, who texts and says
'Hey! Best Friend!'
Love who eats the cookies
You bake and
Comments on each ingredient.
He tells how badly you bake while licking his fingers
And hiding his smile.
Love who lets you doodle on his hands.
Love who sits with you quietly for hours
And you never get bored.
Love and you often say the things in unison
And he exclaims,
'We said the same thing!'
Love who accidentally wears
The same color as you do.
Love who loves another girl
And you love another man.
Love who isn't meant for marriage and children.
Love who isn't meant to get lost
In bills and chores.

Love which is just a call away.

Love who is from another state.

Love who doesn't spend much time with you.

But Love is always as it is from day one whenever you think of him.

Love who doesn't need a body and a contract.

But just a heart and a soul.

Japanese Knotweed

My Love was a Japanese knotweed.
I was startled with his beauty,
And struck by his smile.
His soothing words surrounded me with gaiety.
For him I was ready to walk
A thousand miles.
Like a bee I was attracted to his creamy blossoms.
His love planted on my soul was
Dense yet hollow.
And on his heart-shaped leaves I wrote
My name million times so.
But while I was falling in love more and more,
I forgot
He was my Japanese knotweed.
He started to rule me and
I took it as a ritual of love.
On each command I would say,
Yes Sir!
Slowly, "you-hail and I-obey"
Became a custom.
In all this,
To be loved became an unsaid crave.

When days changed into years,
His roots broke the concrete.
My heart was no longer mine,
But a territory clustered with brown stems.
One spring I found,
My heart was unwanted and disguised.
Done with humiliation,
I decided to dig him out.
I dried its roots and set them on fire.
I watched my love go till it turned into ashes.
As I feared,
It would have grown again.
Since my love was,
Japanese knotweed.

Before We Part

Eyes cry, but then what love is
Without pain, without wait.
To love you is destiny, to lose you is fate.
What angels wouldn't bring, falling in love
And falling apart will get.
To me, you are a saint in a devil's cloak.
Who is meant to travel with me but
With bodies away. We shall lock
Our fingers in each other's hands..
One day.
But then you and I will hear the whistle
Of the departing train.
I might even kiss your lips and
You could even embrace me hard.
Then you will tremble, and I will shiver.
Unwantedly I'll wave you a goodbye.
Our paths will cross again,
But this time we would run into each other
With no fear and no chains.
And we shall let the spring shower on us
The blooms which you always desired
To bring to me on rainy days.

There will be no winters.
But songs of love and hearts' whispers.

Falling in Love Again

He was just right in front of me.
Like my reflection in the mirror.
Had I moved my hand,
I would have touched his face and
Those eyes where love hides.
I looked at him
When he stared away.
Wondering, "Is this a dream?"
I would fix my eyes
At the coffee mug
When I was caught gazing at him.
It's hard to remember
If I was mad at him
For all the heartaches.
But all I can recall is
when he was right in front of me
My faith in "Prayers do get accepted"
Was getting stronger.
But then,
I was too afraid to hold his hand.
What if he was a mirage?
I left my hands empty.

That night, I couldn't sleep.
I was too afraid
To wake up seeing him gone.
I wonder, if I would ever sleep
Even though he is right here.

Dreams

And I dreamt-
Or I started to dream.
When you held me-
Or that was just my belief.
Well I dreamt to walk with you
In forgetfulness
On the seashore somewhere
In a jangling crowd.
But the only sound that would
Hurl us will be of yours and mine
Whispers.
To be warmly saved in your arms,
To see the horizon kissing the sun.
To see the waves embracing shore
Will bring the scarlet hope
On my pale heart.
I dreamt, to see the light
Of the tired city.
Half asleep and
half worrying about insomnia.
I dreamt to touch
The old Budha's sculpture

With your hands.
And to sit under Bodhi's tree
Which belongs to Ashoka.
I wished (though it was a secret before
I wrote this poem)
To move my fingers on your face
With unseeing eyes.
To feel your deep-dark eyes,
Your restless lines on forehead,
And screaming-barren lips.
With my touch I'd take away
The tumult of your heart
And there set you at peace.
I dreamt-
Oh, I dreamt to take you on a boat
And hear the splash of water.
While the journey paves its way
I fill my black soul with
Warmth of yours.
Before this could have happened,
God's angel woke up.
One whose cloak is red
And eyes are burning chambers.
The sky turned grey
And June became January.
It rained and rained
Until I couldn't see you anymore.
Now leans above me is this sky.
Beyond that God sits and stares.
I ask about you and He is silent.

I ask about me and He laughs.
If it's a dream, then wake me up.
But whom shall I ask this favor from?

Broken Union

I am going into an abyss of loneliness.
I am moving out of
The house
That I once thought was my home.
I am leaving my first love
With love still in my heart
And love still in his heart.
The breakup is more like
Breaking up of the walls of our souls
That we built with
Three 'yes's' 10 years ago.
While packing our stuff
And dividing things like two great friends
Our lips locked after many months.
We kissed as the last kiss should be.
And we both went quiet
Contemplating on what a wonderful journey it was.
We went through our photos,
Read our cards and letters.
We laughed at nothingness.
Because somewhere we both knew
We can never despise each other

Despite our differences.
I think this is the thing about
First love.
It is empty of hate, agony and regret.
Our family and friends
Ask us why?
And all we say
Please accept us
Like you always did.
You might see us again
Without being in contract
And you might find us hugging each other
On New Year's Eve.
Do not frown.
Do not bring your wisdom.
Let our friendship stay with us
Because we already have lost too much.

24 Aug 2018

The scorching sun which is
Burning my body and
Peeling off the skin
Is not as painful as
The touch I crave for-
The touch of
One who held my hand
And allowed me
To carve my name on his palm
Like a pagan ritual.
(It brought chills to soul
Yet it was an affirmation
That the silent prayers would be
Heard.
His name is my reward
And my name followed by his is
All what I want.)
Before I could have asked
If he could take part
In my pagan ritual
We parted
To see another Mount Vesuvius-

But now it is just my heart
Buried under the ashes.
It was only I who exploded
When the earth shook,
Melted me in lava
And put me to sleep.
When I woke up,
He was gone.
I survived
To breathe the smoke and live
With fissures on my eyes.
The words are no longer
Helping the lungs which are
Urging to scream.
The insomniac nights are now
Companions of nightmares
Where the ghosts drag him
Away from me.
I wake up panting and wishing
I could snatch him from the world
And leave him not for even God.
Or if only I were entombed
Under the ground of Pompeii
Before falling in love.
24 Aug 79 AD

A Toast

We are the strong ones,
Fighting the maelstrom
That is reckoning our hearts.
We are combating the abrasive pain
That is exploding our souls.
We who are holding the disappointments
On the right palm
And brutal love on the left.
Look at us,
How we manage to laugh
On jokes that
Are abstract art.
We who smile
As if an arrow was broken
Before wounding us
In a battle.
I raise a glass of
Red wine and toast to us!
To the brave ones!
To the fighters!
To us who won't give up!
To us who won't let

Negative energies,
Failures,
Broken hearts,
Poverty,
Shattered dreams, and
Incomplete plans
To drain us.
We won't let the dark
Overshadow us.
We will hold our independence
And sing the peace song.
Because once upon a time
Some wise man said:
"This too shall pass"

Love as if..

Love sounds like a curse when there are zillions of people out there, and you choose to love that one person who can never be yours. Love is called cruel when there are many out there dying to have your attention, but your eyes look for only one person who would never love you back. I call it a trial. I call it a process in which our weaknesses become our strengths. It is to love persistently without demanding love. It is to learn to be happy for what you have without complaining. When you love, be loud! Be honest! Be compassionate! At the end what matters is you loved genuinely, and you loved not to force them to love you back. Love because it makes you happy! Love as if it's your religion!

Ode to a Lost Lover

If they see your eyes turning into
Deep blue ocean
And the Starry Night
Of Picasso-
If they see your face
Turning into dusk,
Tell them not to fear.
Tell them it is nothing but
A woman
Whose insanity was no less than
A witchcraft-
Whose love was unfathomable
And in a flash
You were under her spell.
But it was more than a spell
Because when she placed her lips
On all the parts of your body,
You found your skin, heart and soul
Deceiving each other.
Each one wanted her more from the other-
But then the feather that was carrying you up in the sky,
Hit the ground and

Left you somewhere between the
Approaching Gothic hands of
A dead tree.
Who brought you back home?
You don't remember,
But you do remember,
Her last kiss on your lips before
You could have replaced her
With the beauties who were
Talk of the town.
Your eyes are nothing,
But the reflection
That someone once
Loved your scars, flaws and purity
Without wanting anything back.
And your dusk-face is
Longing for the night
When you had her
Mysterious existence
Ready to perish in your arms
And willing to have a
permanent home inside your heart.

I Carry You

I can't take you home,
Yet I feel you are home.
My mansion.
My palace where walls welcome me.
Your falling-bricks
Drop into my lap,
And I pick them up
Slowly.
Bit by bit.
I kiss them softly
Wishing to touch your soul.
I carry you in the bell jar,
While your breaths are locked inside
A bottle.
Knowing I mustn't love.
Knowing we will end up
Setting the world on fire.
Knowing the star-crossed lovers
Is not just a thing.
But still,
I can feel your lips on my forehead
Dancing and rejoicing

That they had me for a day,
And my lips burning
For not leaving enough of me on your
Heart.

Transitory

I wonder how
The sun can give
all its light to the moon
And disown it
The next day?

Love Them

Give love to them,
And show them the art of loving.
Express love,
Say it,
Sing it,
Write it or
Paint for them.
And then if they play for you
Silent movies,
They send you an empty album,
A broken cassette,
Or maybe they just vanish inside a
Translucent hive,
Then step aside gently.
It's okay if our kisses,
our shape, our eyes, our touch
are a puff of smoke
To them.
They are not obliged to love us.
They are not obliged to stay
And watch the sky falling on us.

Stolen Moments

Where am I?
After crossing everything from the list of love.
Love made in the moments stolen from life.
Love grown out of the seeds of amaranth.
It was surely nowhere from this world
But maybe a heaven beyond.
But where am I now?
Am I floating on the Dead Sea?
Or am I lost in the corn fields and
Neither finding a way forward or back.
Am I now the sun burning for a day?
Or am I the moon who is nothing but
Surviving on a borrowed light?
Am I a lover or a beloved?
I am a fountain of water
And I'm a thirsty traveller.
I am prohibited to drink from my own fountain.
I am vanishing from my heart's desire
And the soul's eyes.
Because eyes ask for a harbour.
They want a shore,
And I can't give them anything

Nor I can deny them.
So I hide inside a temple
Which lost the worshippers long ago.
Because I know this feverish love,
The blazing bones,
The exquisite eyes,
The daring lips
Won't settle down.
They will keep orbiting the sun
To find their leap year back.

Fragile

The promises are strong
When made
And fragile when broken.
Last week while lying in your arms
I asked you
Will you always remember me,
And you answered
You will never lose me.
But did we see this coming?
The silence,
The isolation,
The separation?
I want to scream,
I miss you!
I want to chalk on the walls of this
Mad town, "Come back!"
But you are not here to hear my voice
Nor you would read my words.
So today I put a lock
On the promise bridge
Whispering,
"I will always remember you."

BLOOMING SCARS - 51

Spring in Love's Autumn

Can you see
The trees changing colors?
The leaves turning green and it seems like
It took them a decade to forget that yellow shouldn't be their forever.
Well, you were my wild summer,
You reminded me that I still have seeds of love
Left on my skin.
Maybe you were the rains that fall before summer takes over autumn.
A rain that makes sure that field brings the blooms out of the earth.
The last kiss when our lips met for a final goodbye was supposed to bring the melancholic air.
But I'm surprised that it was more of a dawn
Bringing to my dark eyes the joy of a morning.
Where would I go now?
I have stopped all my attempts to escape now
Because even though you didn't have much to say,
You gave me love-
How and when..

I don't know.
You said you don't know either.
But even when I belong nowhere,
Somehow you have marked on my heart
That wherever I would go,
I'll always belong to you.

Prayers

I was told that some prayers don't get rejected
And others which do
Will be compensated for greater blessings in heaven.
I pray to have you
Despite knowing
This prayer will be rejected.
But then I want you in all the heavens that God
Has to offer-
In this life you are hers,
But in next life I won't leave you for angles even-
And when this thought crosses my mind
I whisper,
How is it possible?
He doesn't even want me.

Heart is at Home

You ask me not to fall in love with you
For we won't last forever.
We have no past, present and future.
We don't belong to
The months on a calendar
Or even the seconds in a clock.
And I assure you
That I'm not in love-
For love is a state
Where one dreams of waking each day
Next to the person they love.
Love demands to grow old together.
Love asks to sign a contract.
Love often compels to dream of a garden
Echoing with laughter of children
Who are a beam of a promise
Made before one says "I do!"
I don't love you
Because this world is too small to
Fit what I hold for you.
I do not wish a lifetime to love you
Or an eternity to look into your eyes.

I dream of nothing-
I just want to caress the dreams you hide
Between your faded smile.
I want to kiss away the sea from your lips
And leave a fountain of honey there.
I want to touch your back
And count the vertebrae in your spine
And make my way to your mind.
I want to feel your skin
And absorb your fragrance.
I want to listen to your heartbeat,
So the sound of it be my companion
When I am drowning in rising waves.
I want to pour you rich red wine
And drink from your lips.
I want to dance with you to
'with or without you'.
I want to whisper the words of Pablo in your ears
And I want you to sing to me a song of hope.
I know moon and stars are too much to ask for,
I know God hasn't written a night in our fate
When we could witness nebulae while holding each other.
But I know at least He has written an hour in which my soul will travel inside yours
And hold it, and those 3600 seconds
Are greater than any eternity I spend without you.
But you ask
If it's not love, then what is it?
I say,
Why to care for a title

When the heart has already found its way.

The World Remembers Us

> We have parted,
> But world still write
> Yours and my name
> Together.

My Darling

Far from you
I can hear your voice echoing in my ears
Like church bells calling the worshipers.
The chanting saints
Announcing the words of God
Among the walls painted with
Stories of prophets and decorated with gemstones.
I feel you as if
You are a city who has seen
The good times and bad times,
And now it's all green.
You are a talisman
Given to me by a nomad wandering on the streets
And now I'm too scared to keep you
Because you belong to the crowns
Made of gold
While I carry the garland made of jasmines, roses and scars.
The walls of my house are frozen now,
They don't allow me to go out
Because now any place on this earth
Without you is nothing but a prison.

My heart trembles
Because what I have is a separation
Exhibited by love and sorrow,
So what is there beyond this separation?
Agony??
I hope there is a silver lining beyond
The pure dark clouds.
I hope there are meadows beyond this barren land
which echo with your songs.

Dissolving in Ashes

If your words can eradicate
My body from the core,
I wonder what it would feel like
Touching you.

Ode to My Ex Best Friend

There are days when I
Do want to reply to your messages,
Or call you back
And ask you how you have been.
There are days when I miss your mom,
Your siblings who were my family
I certainly miss our long video calls,
The stupid things we talked about,
The meaningless jokes we cracked,
The endless laughter,
The long-awaited annual meetups
And doing everything crazy
That is meant to be done by
Two people who call themselves best friends.
I miss being there for you
On days when your body refuses to be your fort,
And I miss you when I need a shoulder to cry on
Because I miss him.
Yes 'him' where it all started.
But now it's no more about him,
Or you,

Or us.
It's about me
And my heart that I have now fixed with
Washi tapes to makes sure
The world doesn't see the cracks it holds.
I miss myself,
A person who would brag in gatherings
How lucky she was to have you.
I miss telling lies to the world for favors
You never did to me.
Because part of me wanted my side of the world
To love you as much as I did.
Oh I do.. did.. I do..
Darned! I'm stuck between
I love you and I loved you,
And each time the last petal of sunflower
Announces I loved you,
I let the streams of solitude river
Take over my face.
In your last message you said
In every relationship there are fights,
But how shall I tell you
I wish you had fought for me.
And how shall I tell you
Regular relationship fights
Don't cost a life.
It's a miracle that I am alive
But the undelivered letters I wrote to you
Are turning into ashes
On my kitchen stove.

Soul Communicating with Body

The cold summer nights-
Yes-
Chilled, dark and haunting.
When there's no whisper
No footsteps.
When you sit on your desk
With a suicide note
Written and rewritten a zillion times.
With pills in one hand,
You stare at the name
Whom the letter is addressed.
My dearest, my love,
My life..
And before you grab a water bottle
You ask yourself,
Will he attend the funeral?
Will he come to give
Me a final kiss?
Will he run to see me
For one last time?
Flashbacks!

You are in his arms,
He is brushing your hair,
You are feeling his face with your fingertips,
He is whispering in your ears
Please don't ever leave me.
And you don't answer.
You smile
Because you knew you wouldn't
Dare to lose him.
As to you he was the world.
In fact, he was the sun
And you moved around him
As he were a god
And you the cursed worshiper
Whose prayers never got accepted.
Flashbacks continue.
The life he chose for himself slowly
Started to take him away from you.
You panicked!
You shivered!
You yelled!
You cried!
You screamed!
You fought!
You pushed him away!
And he who had only seen you
As a perfect Chinese vase
Couldn't see you in shards.
He didn't know how to
Fix a broken glass

So he ran away.
And by the time you reached the door
He was gone.
Darn!
Here you are!
Breathing in a body-
That is lying
In a mortuary.
You don't dare to close the door
Because
What if..
What if tomorrow he comes back
What if by now he has learned
The art of loving
And never letting go.
What if
He has realized that
Love is worth fighting a war.
So you keep the pills back.
You tear another goodbye letter.
But I who is seeing you from a corner
Fears
What if
One day-
You will believe
He is not coming back.
Will you kill me?
Will you not give me a chance to live
And to be loved
Once again?

It's All Possible with Love

> With love
> As deep as sea
> And vast as the sky,
> You can paint the world
> Even if you are
> No artist.

Shajarat Al Hayat- The Tree of Life

Last night,
The four glasses of alcohol,
Spending hours looking at beach
And a tiring walk to catch the cab
Couldn't make me sleep.
Your breath in my lungs,
Your lips painted on my face
And then the thought
One day I must hold you in my arms
Kept me awake.
I do not wish to die now
Without leaving
Tint of love on your body-
So that when you walk in heaven,
My love scintillating like
Rainbows
Brings you
To the tree of life
Where I shall be waiting for you.

Soberly Drunk

You come back
Once in a while to see
What you have left behind.
I would never
Give you a pleasure to
See the wrecked soul
Who was broken, torn apart
And crushed by you
In the name of love.
But let me tell you
You have left behind a 'cold heart'
Who breaks everybody who approaches it.
They say damaged people either end up damaging others or keep damaging themselves.
I have chosen former
Just like you.
I break everyone who approaches me.
And the air told me you are curious why I have
Peeled my old skin.
I have changed my hair into purple-
I have undressed my wounds
And have pierced them with gemstones.

So that each touch of yours
Can hide beneath the glitter-
Any fragrance of you on my skin
Must go away with new cells.
I am leaving everything behind
And embracing things
You hated most.
Look what you have done-
You have taught me how to drink
And stay sober.

Shelter

Everything in love
Feels so right.
Love alone can
Make you feel
Protected in a nest.

Set Yourself Free

Don't force yourself to love people you hated some time ago. Listen carefully to your heart. Does it still hurt? Does it want them back? Does it contain the same love for them? If the answer is no then congratulations, you are healed! Now don't peel the wounds. Don't visit the memories. Bygones be bygones. It's okay to cut the cord completely, and that doesn't make you a bad person. It's okay if you are cold to someone who once caused you a terrible trauma, and that doesn't make you a villain. Do yourself a favor, pray for them every day. Pray may they be happy, and pray your heart be at peace.

Teach Us The Art of Growing

All our lives we tell our daughters to wait for someone to bring roses while what we should be doing is giving them seeds and teaching them the art of growing one's own garden.

Reborn

I was 11 when I experienced death.
Death that brings mourning in a house.
Death that leaves you with questions.
Death that teaches you
Human bodies are meant to be cold.
Death that preaches you God is one.
Death that explains your life is transitory.
Death that opens the doors of heaven and hell.
Death that scares you to sleep alone.
Death that makes you unafraid of cemeteries.
Death that gives lifetime lessons.
Death that tells you wearing black doesn't make any difference.
Death which is not defined by a grief period.
Death that warns you everyone is sooner or later going to leave.
Death that shows you to tie your own shoelaces.
Death that builds you as a person with no choice.
And you become someone who wouldn't care
If it is pink or blue.
If it is broccoli or fish.
It is cotton or silk.

If it is science or literature.
Experiencing death at young age
Grows you up before the time.
But I who acquired the thousands years of learning
After touching the graves of my loved ones,
Forgot pain and how to stand it
After falling blindly in love.
I forgot that I was stronger than a heartbreak,
I forgot that only death can part us is just a phrase
I forgot that humans are meant to leave
I forgot that losing someone to death
Hurts more than a betrayal.
I FORGOT! I FORGOT! I FORGOT!
I forgot how I survived in a house
Whose walls turned cold
After the funeral of those who started to love me
Before I was born.
And I forgot that sometimes pain is bestowed upon us for a trial.
Getting my heart broken
Left me in denial.
Denial that love we trusted can be wrong.
Denial that person we love the most can be unjust.
Denial that vows can be lies.
Denial that we can be used in the name of love.
Denial that we saved the broken person so they would save us back.
Denial that there can be a demon inside an angel's cloak.
And in those denials, I was filling the air in a balloon by constantly begging him to

Stay! To come back! To be mine! To accept me!
Forgetting that I was a survivor of typhoons.
Forgetting that him changing overnight
Wasn't my mistake.
Forgetting that I loved him enough and he was ungrateful.
Forgetting that I am important too.
Forgetting that I deserve to be happy.
And forgetting disloyalty of one person
Mustn't make me judge 7.5 billion people out there.
And today I embrace myself
I tell myself it's time to rise again.
I love the scars on my heart.
I kiss my wrist where the gravest wound lies
Because what death couldn't teach me
Betrayal has.
I am stronger than yesterday
Because I have found
Those who love us
Can be touched by death
And those who are meant to break heart
Cannot be stopped
With any amount of love.

One Day

And there
In the world out there,
All our whys
Will be answered.

Questions

Questions can be harsh.
Questions can be scary.
Questions are anxiety.
Questions are shadows that creep inside the bedroom from under the door.
Questions are wicked.
Questions aren't beautiful.
Questions are dark
And they can turn off the lights.
But questions are knowledge when Nat Geo says be curious.
Questions are innocent when they come from children
Questions are wisdom if they make you wonder what enlightenment is.
And questions that do no good to
soul, body and mind
Can burn us to ashes.
Question:
When will you get married?
We do wish to tell you that this is a reason we don't see much of our relatives.
Question:

Oh! ten years in a marriage and why no children?
How shall we tell you what it feels
Each time we throw a test with just a single line on it.
Then you question if money is being invested
In bringing an offspring who you wouldn't even care to see.
And we would never tell how painful the results of failed IVFs have been.
Question when you ask, "When we will get a job?" And we wish to chalk on universities' walls
DEGREES DON'T COME HERE WITH A JOB GUARANTEE
Question when we who have lost dads are asked
"Oh! Who pays the bills?"
We wish our moms wore red capes so their strength could be seen!
Question how a woman can be depressed after giving birth to a new life
We wish they taught postnatal depression in schools.
Your questions make us refuse invitations.
"I have an appointment today."
We lie while lying in bed.
Questions are malicious when they question our identity.
It's for questions the word "introvert" exists.
Questions we avoid because they bring depression
Since not all of us can say on your face
IT'S NONE OF YOUR BUSINESS!
You ask me how we can be happy without kids.
We wonder how we should tell you this happy-go-lucky fights the storms at night.

You ask why a husband makes breakfast.

And we google to find: "Does it break the marriage contract?"

You question how a woman can jump from a plane without her man.

And we want to scream
MASCULINITY CAN BE ACROPHOBIC.
Questions and questions
For which we don't have answers.
Because we are air
And now wish to be free.
Leave the questions
For children.
For scholars.
For scientists.
For philosophers.
Questions that are arrows
Kill us slowly.
Allow us to be humans
Not battlefields.

Words I Believed in

And sometimes I wish to call him. Not to know if he still loves me or did he ever love me, but to ask did he really mean when he said he wished he had met my mother or he really loved my brother, or how much positive change I brought in him. Sometimes it's not love we care to lose but words we believed in.

Confession

I will make a confession today. Yes, a confession which I never whispered to my shadows. But first let me tell you how it started. It began years ago when I was a colorful painting not like Mona Lisa with few colors and too much mystery. I was Pollock's modern art. An art with life. An art with so many colors and each color entailing life, passion and fight. I was a love yet too afraid to fall in love. I was bold yet too prudent to give my heart away. And then I met you. No, let me put it rightly, You, came into my life. You chose to stay despite my persistence. You started flying around me like I was the only nectar in your life. I avoided, I ignored, and I stitched my heart which was slowly falling in love with you. I belonged to someone else and I had no control over my life, but secretly I became rebellion. I chose you over him. I broke the norms and stood for you. I left the one who was chosen for me by society and I gave you my all heart. I uncovered my soul layer by layer. I forgot all the pride and arrogance I was famous for. I started sharing with you all those hidden secrets and slowly I was transparent to you. And I confess I love you more than I ever loved anyone. You are Sun just like your name soothing and burning me at the same time. But now after all this time it seems I was just a friend to you. A friend with whom you can laugh. A friend good enough to hang out with. It seems you were obsessed only with my beauty and you tried to win me so you can envy your friends. You say they don't believe you how drenched I am in your love. For heaven's sake! I am not a challenge or trophy! I have buried my ego just to love you and hold you till my last breath. Why don't you see the spark in my eyes when I see you? Why can't you notice my fading smile when you say I can never fall in love? Why can't you see I am losing myself bit by bit in your love? Love me before I become Mona Lisa with pale colors and charade smile.

Despite the Efforts

> We women spend lifetime
> Carrying the lessons on our spines
> Passed on to us by our mothers
> Only to find
> We don't have enough to be called
> Good wives.

Question Loneliness

Being lonely
Is not corroding.
You can always find a home
Inside you.
You can always see
The sun setting down
Or the sun rising from the East.
And you can always look at it
As an art hanging on the museum walls.
But if you say
Loneliness is venomous,
Then ask the child waiting in orphanage
For years to be found.
They look at the door everyday
to be opened to the new world.
If you ask of loneliness,
Then ask an old man
Shattered and decayed
Who lost a partner
Because god decided to test him
By taking everything, he ever loved.
Now he sits at the door and

Looks at the people with their heads
Fallen into pit while holding
The hands of their children
Walking in loop.
He asks god
What is it to have home?
If you ask of darkness
Of this prison bar
Which some call life
Then look at the woman who loved
With all that is left of her
Only to be abandoned on the roadside
For another woman.
Ask her
How does she hide her red eyes
From her mother.
How does she keep her chin up
As if life is such a fair circus.
Ask of loneliness from the bodies
Who are created just to fill lust
While their hearts burst.
While their souls shatter
For loveless empty ghosts.
Ask of loneliness from those
Who are taken to the garden of rose
Only to be told
That garlands do not belong to coals.
Ask of loneliness from those who are betrayed
And they find the courage to trust
The entity of love but sooner

They become skeletons in the closet.
Asks of loneliness from jasmines
Which wither and decay.
Ask of loneliness from poems
That are never to be read.
Ask the love
That was defined by laws.
Ask.. ask..
Ask the heart the that is taken home
Only to be crushed
And left without a sound to mourn.

Right Timings

Does healing hurt? Yes! It hurts, but it hurts so one could be free. Staying in pain and not making an effort to heal is more hurtful. First, you are allowing yourself to get hurt for nothing; second, you are stopping yourself from receiving the miracles that the universe has to offer. So here is an advice: walk away when it's not working, be it a relationship or a job. Don't take more than what you can bear even if you have fears of survival. You would question your strength to live without your toxic job since you think right now it's your only source of income. You will be hesitant to leave the relationship that is causing you pain because you are afraid that you might not be able to hear I-love-you's. You're counting the minutes they spent with you more than the hours they weren't there for you. But trust me, God has His own way of providing you with the best. The way to the exit door from a toxic room might look scary, but once these steps are taken with heavy steps and pounding heart, your soul will find home within! Your heart will heal!

My Methadone

He is the worshipper of
Silence,
Solitude
And
Serenity.
And I love
The Sound,
His company,
And
The hurricanes.
To him love is best
When spoken without words.
To me the love he puts in his words
Is my methadone.
I wish
He speaks more
Because he doesn't know
We are running out of time.
The sun is always in a hurry to set down
Like the love
Rushing out of home.
Embrace me,

Before the night
Swallows my soul.
Whisper words of love,
Because tomorrow I may not
Hear.

It's Clear Now

Was that love?
Was I in love with an illusion?
Now that the hues are gone
The sky is clear
The sea is blue
And the rosy glasses of love are no more
On my eyes
I realize
I wasn't in love with him
But myself.
I was in love with my idea of him.
Now when I have grown my own garden
Of jasmines
I can see
Love wasn't pink.

Dollhouse

When I was six,
I went to my neighbor's house
And asked a girl there to play with me
Dollhouse.
She sat down,
But without a doll.
Without a house.
I set the things,
I spread a small picnic blanket.
I placed tiny cups filled with water,
Put the dolls on the floor.
On tiny plates I kept
Chocolate bar.
We had an imaginary tea party with some cake.
And when it got over
I started to put things back
In the basket
The girl started to cry.
I kept waiting.
I kept sharing.
I would try to leave,
She would cry again.

Then it started to get dark outside.
I packed everything,
Gathered the courage and stood,
But when I looked behind
There was nothing.
Nothing that girl shared.
It was my doll
And my toys.
I never went to play with her again.
Now at 31,
I look back and see,
I again played dollhouse with someone,
But this time
Doll had a name: *Relationship*.
What was he contributing?
It took me while to understand that
I wasn't in love but
Emotionally trapped.
I decided to leave several times,
But he would end up hurting himself,
And my guilt would stop me.
But then one day,
I found he was as empty as his words.
He was a poet but without love.
He was a magician without a wand.
He was a healer without herbs.
He was a star without the sky.
And when I stopped giving,
He left.
Because there was nothing that belonged to him.

And now this man who sits across me
Looking at me while I type this,
Waiting for me to sip a coffee
That he just made
I tell myself,
What a blessing it is to fall into nothingness
Before sipping a glass full of wine.

Warriors

We are daughters of warriors.
Warriors who carried us inside their wombs
And taught us the first lesson,
Carry your own weight
With pride,
With a smile.
So how can you just
Give up
Without even picking up
a sword?

Depression

It has two faces
The happy one that the world knows
And the sad one that no one can understand.
On happy days it's perfect sunny side up egg,
The well brewed coffee, the clear blue sky,
Jasmines on the writing table, the sound of wind chimes.
And on the *sad* days-
Which are not sad because
Sadness makes you numb, sadness makes you feel sorry,
Sadness asks you to take a break, sadness allows you to watch a movie or listen to a song
No matter how sad it is.
The days I am talking about
Are called depressed days in my world.
There you smile at work, laugh with your friends
And tease your family.
But you find the bathroom an asylum.
In those four walls you hold the screen of your phone and desperately look for any one contact number who can be a savior, but you don't call
Because calling is not what depressed people do.
You text and tell, you need help and you get a reply

"You were just fine in the morning"
You text a second person who calls back
Hesitantly you answer and you hear them loud.
Because they studied psychology at the university
For 2 credit hours and now they find you
A guinea pig and themselves a god of mental health.

They remind you how you are going to ruin your reputation.

They scold you that this is all because of a drink you had last week.

They tell you had you been a worshipper of God this wouldn't have happened.

You hang up and there you make a final mistake:

You CALL YOUR EX whose fragile ego was waiting for this day!

He puts on the crown, laughs in a mirror
Pats his shoulder and blocks you!
Bang!
There! You unaware what to do next
Collapse on the bathroom floor
Which doesn't swallow you
And you ask the lord whom you don't talk much
to order the ground to bury you.
What does depression look like?

1. Palpitations
2. A constant alarm that something bad is going to happen soon
3. Pulling hair

4. Digging nails in one's skin
5. Drawing ribbons on one's arms with sharp razor
6. Eating everything or nothing at all because normal is not a word for this disease.
7. Crying for hours apparently for no reason
8. Wishing to press the stop button of the world
9. Pushing away everyone you love
10. Locking oneself in a house for days
11. Making other people laugh
12. Doing your work on time or not doing anything at all
13. Shopping the best unwanted stuff
14. Helping the ones in pain

You see the symptoms of depression are so confusing,
Imagine what the brain would look like.
It is half Picasso and half Pollock,
It is half mud and half star,
It is a string of a broken guitar
And a key of a brand-new piano.
And to talk about depression
Is to draw out an old bag from under your bed,
As you drag it out the dust goes into your throat and nostrils.
You cough you sneeze, but since the bag is out
You decide to dust it.
And your friends and family who just came to your room to wish you birthday
After seeing the room full of dust leave.
Now the bag is open, you decide to take help

Prozac and Symbyax, and some more pills.
You clench your teeth; in an empty room you scream.
Because every medicine has its side effects,
But slowly when you start to get better
You see the world looking at you
With judgmental eyes.
When you call wrong a wrong
They remind you of your past.
When you call right a right
They call you insane.
They bestow you with titles
And you regret telling the world
That you needed help.
But one day
At 3 in the morning
When all is coming back
You get a message from someone
You have never met
Which says
Thank you for sharing your story.
Thank you for saving my life.

Too Late

One day
It will be too late to
Confess love.
To apologize.
To say, "You are beautiful".
To tell you want to come back.
One day it will be too late
For the sun to set
And the moon to rise.

The Song of Demons

Am peeling off my skin
Hoping to get rid of
The thorns of anxiety
The isolation
The dead dreams
Lying in my atoms and
Turning into cancer.
Am living a life
That isn't mine.
That can't be mine.
An illusion
That is meant to be broken
The shadows that are supposed to eat me soon.
I am living in a skin
That is borrowed from the walking
Ghosts.
This life
Is the life where demons drink blood
To survive.
And they are now the parasites
Eating me bit by bit
Slowly..

Softly..
Painfully..
In silence..
Among the crowd..
In solitude..
In noise..
These parasites are taking my soul
And leaving the marks,
The scars,
The claws on my arms
Demanding me to die.
Urging me to jump from 6 floor.
These whispers
Do not leave me
When I am in my beloved's arms,
Or in hot shower,
Or dancing on a floor,
Or sitting next to an old lover's grave.
These demons
Demand
Life
Like a Viking ritual
That asks for power.
And I have lost
All reasoning
All power
All faith to
Deny them.

Save Thyself

A day will come when you will be asked by the universe to make some brave choices. A choice to choose respect over heart. A choice to save your own heart than mending someone's. A choice to focus on lessons than losses. Listen to me, you will always find plenty of opportunities, love and success, so if this is a defeat then take it! Walk away from things which are underestimating you. Walk away from people who are taking you for granted. Shut down all the doors which are unhealthy for your soul because you deserve so much more! You have a long path to travel, so don't drain yourself for people who won't even be there tomorrow.

Girl with Purple Hair

I will never believe a girl who would say that
There's no story behind her purple hair.
Because no one can go on and take a risk of destroying something
Which was dearly loved by one's mother
Whose touch lives on each strand.
Something the girl loved because a traveler
She gave her heart to, would brush it while dissolving in her deep brown eyes.
And I am sure
If that lover dares to come back,
He would have the guts to ask
'why would you do it?'
Why would you just paint something beautiful
With such odd color.
Because those who set the souls on fire
Can't see why they mustn't
Destroy humans.
There is a deep connection with
Badly done hair
And a broken heart.
I remember cutting them short

When my mother died.
I remember turning them into
Cubicles which looked no closer to
Picasso's reading girls.
I have punished my hair several times
For nothing .
For nothing that my body is responsible for.
I am not guilty for loving a man who was
Just giving me love
To take the pleasures form atoms and molecules
That make the mass of my body.
I am not guilty of loving a damaged man
When I knew no human
Must be a rehabilitation center.
I am not guilty for kissing the lips
That tasted the matte
From someone else's lips
Soon after I left them.
Yet I punished my body,
My hair, my skin, my heart and my entity.
Because all this time I kept asking:
Where did I go wrong in loving him?
What could have I done that would have made him stay?
What was not in me that made him look at some other woman?
How can he hold on to an hour's fight rather than a zillion days of love?
How can he say I suffocated him when he would make me wait for hours and days?

And that wait was like a plastic bag wrapped around my face
And I breathed counting seconds for him to come
And pinch a hole so I could let air in.
And I punished myself
For things I wasn't responsible for.
When I went to salon
And told the hairdresser to cut my hair
So short that no man ever dares to look at me,
He screamed and spent 30 minutes convincing me that men would stare at me anyway.
But I hurt myself forgetting that
His departure has opened the doors of
Strength and courage
That I wouldn't have acknowledged in his presence.
Now this girl who is taking psychology with me says
Her purple hair has no story,
I smile.
Because we all have punished ourselves for the sinners who are not even guilty.
Because people who break heart
Are called criminals in no constitution of the world.

New World

If I could set the world
which I see through my daughter's eyes,
I will keep it simple.
A place where colors survive
With the tint of trust, truth and tolerance.
Where she would be able to walk
As smoothly as the summer breeze.
A place where her dreams grow into the gardens of life.
Where love is meant to be love,
Where hate is not the other side of the coin.
Where asking for the rights is not a taboo.
Where touch doesn't mean leaving the bruises.
Where promises mean courage.
Where pink is not fragile but power.
Where body doesn't define beauty.
Where wings are not meant to be cut down.
If I could give my daughter the world to live in,
I will give her the world
where strength doesn't need to come from heartbreak.
A world where faith in relationships is not lost.
Where she is not cursed
for her brother's, father's or husband's deeds.

Where she is a morning song,
Not a word to be used as a curse.
If I could give my daughter the world to live in,
I will give her
the poems of Maya, paintings of Frida and
a heart of Khadija.
And I will tell her,
know the women from their first name
Because it took them ages to build it.

To Phoebus

The hues on our face
And yours and mine black dress-
The clear blue sky
Are asking if our souls are
Lost lovers found.
Who were you to me
In past life?
Who will I be to you
In the next life?
Time knows.
God knows.
The sunflower in your garden knows.
The jasmine near my window knows.
The ocean knows-
Phoebus knows-
Cosmos know.
Stars know.
What metaphysics cannot answer,
Our souls can.
So let me hold your hand
And sit in silence,
Before the jasmines wilt,

Ocean dries, and
Phoebus runs out of words.
Let me take the sad atoms
That are holding you tightly
And drowning you.
And I will replace them
With the pixie dust
And some magic touch.
So when we part
I carry you in my soul-
You carry me in your heart.

To Old Me

To the old me
Who I can never be again.
Dearest 17-year-old girl,
I look at your photos and recall
Your laughter that would echo in the theatres.
On the buses.
In restaurants.
In libraries.
You would laugh at the silliest jokes.
You would laugh as if life
Was a carnival and you would never come out of it
And visit the alleys of a city
That is drowning in sorrows.
I miss how you would climb the trees,
Knowing you would fall
And break your bones.
And you did fall and still laughed
While holding the limbs.
I smile when I think how you
Jumped into the sea
Knowing you couldn't swim, and
You didn't care when people who ran to save you

Later yelled at you.
You laughed more.
Time flies.
They say.
They are right.
You lived your life as if there's no tomorrow.
One night you woke up and booked yourself
A scuba dive.
When your friends freaked out
You went on and skydived.
You weren't afraid of anything, were you?
You loved. You flirted.
You lived life-
And you made life to love you,
But then..
When you hit thirty
Where everyone had recovered from a heartbreak
And living the life of a clerk.
You got your heart into trouble.
You loved him and slowly
You forgot to love yourself
Because his love was enough.
But love didn't work because
Miracles don't work
For a rider who doesn't have a horse,
And for a warrior who has no sword,
And for a virgin woman praying for a child,
And for the moon who doesn't want the sun,
And for the forest whose birds have been killed,
And for the valleys that have been abandoned,

And for a dead one who is lying in a casket,
And for a boy who has already jumped from the 22nd floor.
And for a hope that is buried with bones,
And for a shipwreck that kissed the seabed 200 years ago.
Love didn't work for you
Because you were too loving, too emotional
Too sensitive for a lover
Whose glass was full.
And this too much of "too"
Parted you two.
Oh no! Wait!!!
He departed. Quietly.
But here you can hear
The sound of rising waves,
The building getting demolished in the next block,
The volcano erupting in Pinatubo.
But what you can't hear
Is the sound of your laughter.
Because you don't laugh anymore.
You are scared of air,
The rocks,
The waves.
You are too afraid to walk home
Because unconsciously you built
Home inside him.
You are lost-
And I miss you
Dear me.

Together We Will

I know you have painful memories and all that is happening is because of what you went through. Now you think everyone is going to hurt you. You fear you will get pain and tears if you love someone. I do understand your feelings my friend, but listen, I am with you to fight your demons. I am here to fight with your depression. We are half souls, so let me fight with you. Let me make you believe that not everyone is the same. I want to cosset you, just like you want to care and love me. I am always there for you! I know I am bad at expressing, but that doesn't mean I don't care, or I don't love. You have always told me to hold your hands. Here, today I am asking you to try holding mine. I promise this too shall pass. I promise we will come out of the darkness. I promise you will become stronger and better.

Tale of an Expat

I am an expat
From a country that I miss
When it's too hot to breathe.
I miss it when it rains here
And I can't smell the snacks
Being fried in the kitchen.
I miss when I am on the road trip
And can't find the street food.
I miss when I come home, and there's nobody to ask
Shall I warm the food.
Because the only one to ask that is
a food delivery app.
I miss my country often and when I tell this to my friends there
They question why in the past ten years I have only visited it thrice.
How shall I tell them that this expat
Feels like an outsider
In her own country.
Yes, I feel like a foreigner
When my own family
Can't decide what room to give me.

When they go through all the hustle of
Getting new bed covers, curtains and cushions.
And I want to scream I am no guest so let me feel at home.
I feel like a tourist
When my friends take me out
To expensive luxurious restaurants.
The type of restaurants where not using
Forks and knives are considered a taboo.
It's hard to explain to them that I have had
Enough of English breakfast in these years
And I yearn for simplicity.
I shiver when at parties I am not treated
Like everyone else
And bombarded with basic questions.
Yes those basic boring questions
Like how are you,
How's the day,
How's family,
Sound better in those moments rather answering
How much I earn.
If it's Gucci or Prada
And I answer
It's made in China
The frown of disappointment
Shows up on their face as if I have failed to do
Addition and subtraction sums.
I feel them scanning my old phone
That I haven't updated for years now.
I feel them getting shocked
When they ask if my lips bloom with

Huda or Sephora

And I answer neither.

The dilemma if I am an expat in a country whose passport I do not hold

Or the land where I was born but do not live

Is like a fish being told that it should breathe on a land

And when it goes out of water, its lungs refuse to cope.

The word international pushes me away away away inside the walls which refuse to take me in.

I look at the TV's screen and wonder should I voice out my opinion about the difficulties that my soil faces?

I feel the pain!

I feel the pressure!

I feel the problems,

But I can't tweet about them

And demand justice

As my people's eyes blame me as if I am a soldier

Who has betrayed the battalion.

I can't talk who should be running my country

Because they ask why do I even care when I am not facing any of it.

I see the unrest there, I stay quiet here.

Because I am an outsider.

I don't read newspapers anymore.

I have deleted my Facebook so I don't get to know

What's happening out there.

But then

Last week I was staring at the skyscrapers and noticed

My country's flag swinging in the air.

And I wondered

How long it has been there
Trying to prove that an expat somewhere is still carrying their mother inside their heart.
How dare they try to be patriotic
When they chose to leave the land.
But still, I know
Most of us write a will
To send our corpse back home
Knowing-
We belong nowhere
Knowing it's too late to belong somewhere.

Irreplaceable

Now it doesn't make any difference
if someone leaves roses on my doorstep
or send me my favorite song.
Now it doesn't make any difference if
someone promises forever
or tells me they cannot live without me.
Now it doesn't matter if someone swears to fix my broken heart
or refuses to let me go.
It doesn't make any difference if someone writes poems of love to me
or sends me letters of longing.
For I have seen, found and lost love
that is irreplaceable.
How shall I let someone in
when this heart still refuses to let him go?

In the Air

You are still here.
In this very house where we were supposed to live.
In this house where we thought of raising our children.
You are still here
with all your heart and love for me.
But I come home to a dead body
that is of me lying in bed.
It's rotting now with the pain of departure.
Nobody, nobody can see or smell the dead,
and I walk towards it to touch,
but then I hear your voice
still lingering in the air.
I allow this woman to stay dead.
It was you.
It is you that she wants.
Then how can I bury it?
How can I arrange a funeral for someone
who wouldn't let anyone touch her?

Broken House

This is the thing with me,
broken houses
and broken people always fascinate me.
I start with fixing them up,
and I end up
losing myself.

The Poem in the Times of Corona 1

My quarantined friend
we are parted with numbers,
with time
and with this epidemic.
But you keep my heart warm
with infinite compassion floating inside your soul.
My darling,
it's hard to send you love from a distance,
so I write you poems.
I write you songs.
I write you words of hope.
My faraway friend,
sooner we will be sipping coffee together,
and laughing sitting beside each other.
We will be talking of the universe,
love and miracles.
But till then
This virtual world shall keep our souls
alive.

Empty Mansion

You asked me once
why I am so loving
and I replied love is all I know.
And truth is
I wanted to love you completely,
passionately and ardently.
First I loved your mind,
then your heart.
It was seriatim loving,
where I loved every bit of you,
and in this, I forgot to look around.
I forgot the other arts of life.
Now when you are gone,
I am a vacant mansion with the walls
humming my love songs.
I am still so full of love,
as it was the only art I practiced
when you were here
and I don't know how to fill my
empty house.

I Failed..

There have been many things in life
that constantly pushed me down.
Like math for instance.
I would struggle to pass in the exams.
Then piano lessons,
it was hard to remember the keys.
I managed somehow to impress
the music teacher.
I grew up and found
being a woman was a hard job,
but I learned to perform that art too.
And then when at thirty
I thought I had learned all the arts of life,
you came.
You loved me and I believed you.
Thinking I could read hearts.
But only to find that your love was
your infatuation,
while it became my forever.
For you I was a few seconds,
and to me you became an eternity.
So this time I failed.

I failed to stop loving you.

Human Presence

It's beautiful to be someone
who checks on others constantly
if they are fine,
but then
it's also living inside a grave
deep down inside the ground fire pit
where there's no one to talk to.
No one who asks,
"Are you alright?"

We Will Heal

One day we will heal
and look back and smile.
We will be friends again
and we will cherish the moments.
We will write history with our adventures.
One day we will go back to being
a gang of
mad-headed people.
We will laugh,
we will smile.
We will talk.
We will stay up all night
and talk as if we have never been fools
to lose our friendship.
We will live to see the day
when our children will share
the same bond as we do.
The tree of friendship
will grow again,
but till then
I must heal.
You must wait.

He must forgive.

Love Desires

I want you to be a wildfire
and take me inside you.
I want you to be my black hole,
so I disappear in you.
you are my Narnia door
leads me to to the moon
through your love.
I am your hourglass
hoping to turn the time into infinity.
There shall never be
enough words to describe my love.
There can never be enough seconds
to love you.

Depression Hits Again

Is it isolation that is forcing me to pick the long avoided Seroxat again?

Is it missing the feeling of being wild that is making me sit on the bathroom floor and cry?

Are these the days where I expect people to be more considerate, but all I see is that they just take others other for granted?

It's killing me.

I am writing this while getting flooded in my pain.

I am done with the corporate asking me to provide perfection at the time when nothing is perfect.

I am tired of taking orders.

I am tired of explaining to my beloved that depression is killing me.

I am tired of hiding from my friends that how much it hurts when they want my hundred percent attention but fail to be there when I need them.

I am tired of the world around me.

I am fu*king tired of walls crumbling down around me, doors shutting at me and roofs collapsing on me.

I want to give my lover a final kiss,

but I am too afraid to lose him.

I want to leave my job,
but I am too much in love with the smiles
that wait for me.
It's not isolation that is killing me,
it's too much what is expected from me that is draining me.
I wish to sleep,
but my dreams are empty.
And empty dreams,
empty houses
and empty hearts
kill sooner than
any disease.
If it's death,
I take it as an honor.

Home

My home,
My heart,
I want to lie down beside you.
I want my hungry heart
to be filled with your love.
I want my restless fingers
touch your skin and drink you
drop by drop.
I want us,
the two pieces of the same puzzle,
to join and make love so warm
that our skins would melt.
I want to lie down beside you
and drown into eyes.
I want to kiss your spine and smell your neck,
and unfold in your arms
and carry your soul
and let it grow inside me.
My home,
I am an orbit in your love
and I'm lost in you.
Oh take me, and I don't care

if I dissolve in cosmos
or a black hole.

Expedition

You are a covered door
hidden among the forests,
beneath the thousands of years old roots
of juniper.
You are a key to the lost treasure
being searched by the explorers for decades.
A mysterious land which takes away
every object, everything, and every human
who dares to enter inside its territory.
You are a silent route
that leads to an unknown destination.
You are certain there's no traveler
brave enough to set their footsteps on your island,
but I who isn't afraid to lose anything
and all ready for the adventure
slowly desire to discover you
grid by grid.
Scale by scale.

Familiarity

I have known you for years
and if I multiply each second,
and every minute,
you and I have been companions
for an infinity.
But there were doors,
that couldn't have been knocked
and walls,
that were too high to climb.
I could hear you from the other side
while you sang sweet melodies of a deafening silence.
Then one day
we grew wings and decided to escape.
But no matter how far away we flew from each other,
here you are tending my wounds
as if you have been waiting since forever.
and *here* I am,
growing blooms on your scars
as if this is all what life is supposed to be.

Nani's (Grandma) Lessons Don't Work

"Speak, cry your heart out my child,
but don't let silence eat away the love of your hearts."
The next moment I heard sounds
of arguments,
of anger,
of sadness,
of complaints,
but then at lunch
mom was asking dad what he would have for dinner
and he answered, "We will dine out tonight."
They smiled. Nani's advice worked.
Years later
my love was mad at me, so
I sent him long painful messages.
I kept asking him to talk
because nani said
words are stronger than silence,
but nani couldn't live longer to see
love doesn't reside in four walls anymore
but on two continents.

Where if one chooses to shut oneself behind the virtual walls
the other can't do anything to knock them down.

Moment

Love isn't blind
it's a bird
flying high up in the sky
like an eagle
refusing to touch the ground.
Unafraid of wildfires,
unaware of the abyss,
unknown to the depth of oceans.
It's a puff of smoke
one moment here
and another disappearing
with the wind.

Manual

If only
courage had a face,
our sons wouldn't be breaking hearts
of daughters
with silence,
with betrayal,
with abuse.
Courage would be
seeing their fathers
apologizing from women,
fixing the problem,
expressing love
and staying.
I wish one day
someone writes a manual
for our sons
on the art of courage.

Rules

When I was sent on this planet
I saw a family that was living in their own circles
But were forced to stay in a loop.

I was born in a house where people would try their best to avoid each other.

Where having meals together was a punishment.

Where everyone was being a secret rebellion.

I was born in a family who wasn't religious
But they used custom as a religion.

When I turned four, I realized to get the eighth child was not my father's choice.

Women are aware of their physical strength.

Probably that is why my mother decided to bring me into this world.

The world that was not so fair to her and which in years to come wouldn't be fair to me.

What love was like when I was 10?

Leaving the arms of a mother who would blow the longest verses of the Quran every morning on me.

Coming home to an anxious woman who would be waiting with a glass of juice and a meal.

The little heaven, the little love lasted a year.

A home without a mother revealed the shadows
That were hiding behind human bodies.
Her death took away the people and we were no more obliged to stay in the loop.
Some found peace in ashes and smoke.
Others escaped to wine and whiskey-
But we all pretended we lived the life of virtuous Muslim.
But- alcohol was for men,
Cigarettes were for boys-
For women were the four walls, the long piece of cloth and the dreams that burn on the kitchen's stove.
It was okay if a man of the house would spend a night in delicate arms which didn't belong to him.
But it was not okay if a girl would try to hug her father.
It was a man's world where rules were eased for men, by the men.
But - -
The internal war that was eating me away-
The urge to leave such an unfair world started scribbling on my heart.
When sleeping pills couldn't work,
When a bleeding wrist was stopped to set me free-
I decided to write my rules in a transparent diary made from the pages of the universe with an ink from the fountains of unseen heaven.
Rule One:
Being a woman doesn't take away the privilege of
Making decisions!
Decision to study!
Decision to work!

Decision to marry!

Decision to give birth to a child

Decision to divorce!

Rule Two:

God is not an enemy, so I should not fear him!

Now I Love God as if He is a friend since my faith is not a one-sided love affair that needs to be blindly followed but only by the giver!

My faith doesn't encourage breathing in four walls!

I open the holy book and rules are written for both.

I flip the pages and see the Gracious Lord asks us again and again to seek the light of knowledge.

Then there is no such rule that gives men privilege to shut us in the darkness and fill their souls with wisdom.

Rule Three:

To love the child inside me who wasn't loved enough.

So I often tell her!

It's okay if you were born in this fragile body!

It's all right if they judge you!

It's just the dark room with a light button in the corner!

It's okay if mom is not there to turn it on,

eventually you will grow your arms and then I will! I will turn on the light for you!

And I did!

Therefore,

Here I am telling men do not cage us because we know the sky up there is beautiful-

And it does belong to us as well!

On Words

Since the beginning we are told words are powerful.
They are weapons and if used carefully
Then cannons and bombs would get rusted.
Words can start a war
Words can bring peace.
Words can resolve
Words can evolve.
Words can change fate
Words can ignite hate.
Each syllable, each word like atoms and molecules
Make a mass.
Mass of communication-
The emails that run economy, the phone calls that
can find solutions, the paper with a verdict,
a text message of a reminder..
We breathe more in words than oxygen.
We swim in the channel that floats us to other souls who share this planet with us.
Words define us-
They track our roots.
Words have brought people on the roads.
Words have taken down the crowns.

Words are painted on churches' walls to remind us of GOD.

Words are engraved on tombstones to be read at times by none.

Words on a prescription to save life.

Words on the signboards to give warnings.

Words echoing in theaters.

Words flowing in the air waiting to be returned.

Words recorded by NASA in space.

Words said by the dying ones in hospital beds.

Words floating in this room!

Words are saviors.

Words are a hope to see when it's dark.

Words are the engines pulling the train out of the tunnel.

Words are healers if said with care.

Words bring peace in unrest.

Words sometimes test.

Words let us show our best!

If words are in the air, then what makes your love silent?

What makes you hide that which you hold for your beloved?

What stops you from telling them they are important, they are beautiful.

They are loved, they are needed.

Tell them!

Pick the phone!

Make a call!

Text them!

Words are independent of excuses.

Words are not one-way roads.

Words are not just confined to a small device I hold.

Maybe you can express when you meet your love walking down the street.

Or find them sitting in a coffee shop.

It's okay if you are scared to make an eye contact

Pen and paper haven't been extinct yet.

WRITE! SING! SPEAK! PAINT!

Oh God damn it!

Express! Say! Tell them they mean the world!

Or you miss them!

Or your world is upside down without them!

Or the rain, the stars, the sky, the autumn make you think of them!

Or tell them you are mad! You are hurt!

Oh for heaven's sake knock down the walls and wear the garland of words.

Heartstrings need words.

Love needs expression.

Souls do communicate, but poetry is what they create.

So say what you hold because love might be magical,

But words are the magicians.

Poem in the times of Corona 2

How many days has it been like this?
24?
30?
36?
I don't know.
I have lost a count.
But my pupil burn with sleepless nights
That lit coals
In fear of losing abandoned dreams.
And the work which keeps me occupied all day
Brings a shadow of the moon under my eyes.
I'm one of those unsung teachers
Who are struggling to find means to keep our students entertained.
Along with the days of lockdown
We have also lost the count of
Webinars and online trainings we have attended so far.
On a hope this too shall pass
And we will get to touch the stars.
But then right now,
it's me.

My laptop.
My books
And a cat in this 8 by 15 flat.
I walk from my writing desk to my table
Write undelivered letters.
Then I walk towards my bookshelf
and pick a book which was given to me by a lover I lost.
I cry. I keep the book back.
I question God why when I had decided
To go and find my love back,
He locked me.
Then I stand in balcony,
While I look at the sky and pray,
My eyes also worry for my cat
Who wants to jump out and discover the world
Not knowing that jumping is just falling.
And falling brings nothing but broken bones
Like falling in love.
At 9 pm I play music
And set a concert for my neighbors
Who have families,
Netflix and someone to talk to.
I go back.
Shut the window tightly.
I go on Facebook,
Look at him.
Curse myself
Then curse corona
Because before this
I never knew

Love doesn't leave a heart
It creates mansions in.
Tomorrow I am seeing my therapist again on google meet.
The same
4-7-8
Breathing patterns.
Write a journal.
Feel the five senses.
And when she tells me to understand
Fear- Flight and Freeze
All I pay attention to is how beautiful
The alliteration is.
Because now it doesn't make any difference
If I am losing my mind or
My sanity.
I guess
I have lost enough.
But then last night when I had a panic attack on the bathroom floor
And I drank water from the bathtub
And fought for life,
I wished to live one more day to see
This homesickness which I have
In four walls of my home
To end.
I told my cat
I will come out of this.
You will come out of this.
We will come out of this.

The Only Prayer

She had those dark deep eyes and
A never fading smile.
But some faded desires hidden beneath the face powder.
She was a single mom selling body every night.
Knowing the society didn't approve of our friendship
I still wanted the world for her.
I asked her one day what she wanted from life.

"Nothing." She answered with twinkled eyes and broken dreams.

"Prostitutes don't want anything from life. Just not to send us men who treat this body like a beast.

Night goes away and the beast returns home,
But the bruises he leaves behind take weeks to heal.
And without a client I can't pay the bills."

Soulship

When you say
Our *relationship* is beautiful,
I shiver.
I shiver not because you call it beautiful
But you call this
Bond
Or whatever we share
a relationship.
How shall I call it a relationship
When I know
You and I are the
Typical star crossed lovers-
No.. No.. No..
I don't mean we are forlorn because
There is a villain here.
Look at us!
First, there is 5093 kilometres distance between us-
And even if one of us crosses the ocean
Do you think our union can be a reality?
The reality that a church or a mosque
Would turn into *the relationship*?
Second,

I am stuck here in this
Corporate system.
I wake up,
Go to work.
Come home,
Have lunch,
Work again.
Till I no longer keep my
Eyes open.
Till I no longer remember the
Abandoned dreams
I lost in
This cycle of
Wake up, work, sleep, repeat.
Wake up, work, sleep, repeat.
And third,
there you are across the seas
Living the life for others
Between 9 to 5
Or 9 to 6
Or 9 to 7
And sometimes 9 to 9-
And to keep yourself warm
You text me once in a day
"Hey! How are you?"
Now you see
The ship has sunk
And the moss covers it
In greenish layers of
Lovers' dreams

which stink now
Because of possibility of impossibilities.
The charade that
We are lovers for eternity
Keeps me in eerie universe
And leaves me alone
On the buses
At the railway stations
In the theaters.
Because I don't see *us*
Kissing secretly in any of those places.
Because I don't see *us*
Visiting doctors to know
The progress of
Our unborn baby.
I live a busy life
But I sleep in a depressing world
Because no where in future
I see you and I
Sharing the books we talk of, or
Sipping the coffee from each other's mugs
We share the photos of.
No where I see a tomorrow
Where we are making the text message
"I am holding your hands and not letting them go"
A reality.
I know-
Long distance relationship
(which is not a relationship)
Sucks!

But it's beautiful
Because you get to know I am filled with
Sadness even when we are miles apart.
I send you
The poem of Pablo
When you just feel like reading it.
Because you know my day
Ended up like a cigarette butt
And you make sure I sleep with stars on my lips.
The distance doesn't stop me from
Touching your soul
That is eaten up by the wolves
Of stress, anxiety and sadness.
Because you know-
That this bond
Is independent of 5093 kilometres.
Because I know,
I am not so fond of mathematics
So I pick the map
And set it on fire.
I know
We know-
That we have found the pearl of love
From the mysterious ocean.
It's okay if we are apart-
It's okay if our kisses are emojis.
It's all right if the only hug we can give is through
A tiny yellow person with arms open.
This bond
is beautiful because we share

The art, the music, the rain, the loneliness
Through virtual world
And read each other's mind
Better than two people
Sharing the bed.
Because you and I
Are atoms of *us*.
and
It is so beautiful
That I choose to call it
SOULSHIP.

Loud Whispers!

    Whisper love
    As screams are
    Often ignored!

Acknowledgment

All my life, I have met wonderful people and due to my inability to seize love, I eventually lost them. This book is for each one of you who is right now in my life or have gone away. I have never stopped loving you, and this page is a proof that love can survive all the storms. I don't know what I would have been if it weren't for you all.

People often ask me what inspires me to write, and my answer is "everything". Some of these poems are products of people I met on the planes, at the train stations or at hospitals for just a short time while some came out of long meaningful relationships. The poems reflect survival, love and pain and so does the cover. If you look at those flowers carefully, you will see the symbol of strength.

So I want to thank each one of you who touched me with your love and presence. Of course thank you, God! You gave me some beautiful days of my life. You made me believe that it's possible to love and receive love.

Thank you to an amazing man who gave me almost twelve years of his life. You made me believe in myself. You gave me wings that I never knew I had.

Thank you, my wonderful amazing women tribe, and this includes infinite names since world is full of beautiful women. Anum Aquil, Anjum Daniel, Komal Malik, Amber Ahmed, Faryal Syed, Salma Khader, Hiba Abdullah, Maima, Sulakhshana, Sana Tahir, Uzma Gul, Aysegul, my professors, Dr Fouzia and Dr Saba Zaidi I can never thank you enough! You all made me what I am today!

Thanks to my superhero male tribe, and again I am blessed with splendid humans! My mentor Sir Saji Gul, my lovely brother Haroon, my friends Ihtesham, Waqas, Altaf, Amn and Sohaib, thank you for making me believe that the world still has men who support women.

I am sure I am missing many names, thank you my friends, colleagues, family and my readers. I love you all.

Huma Adnan is from Quetta, Pakistan and she started writing when she was 10. She kept her work hidden in a journal until she turned 22 and her teacher discovered her writings and encouraged her to share her work with the world. Since then the journey has never been stopped. Huma is an author of a novel *Once the Birds Fly* and two poetry books. Currently she is living in Dubai and works as an educationist and a coach. Her work can be found on Facebook and Instagram.

SCAN FOR MORE OF AUTHOR'S WORK

www.ingramcontent.com/pod-product-compliance
Lightning Source LLC
Chambersburg PA
CBHW070427010526
44118CB00014B/1938